ACTIVATING GOD'S JUSTICE

THE EMPOWERMENT SERIES

Kingdom infusion books that empower you to live on earth as it is in heaven

Books in the Empowerment series by Jerame Nelson:

Activating the Justice of God

Activating your Spiritual Senses

Activating your Dream Language

Activating God's Power In Your Life

ACTIVATING GOD'S JUSTICE

A closer look at living the
abundant life in God

Jerame Nelson

Living at His Feet Publications
Living At His Feet Ministries
591 Telegraph Canyon Rd. Suite 705
Chula Vista, CA 91910

www.livingathisfeet.org
admin@livingathisfeet.org

ISBN 978-0-9849687-2-5

For Worldwide Distribution, Printed in the U.S.A.
1 2 3 4 5 6 7 8 9 10 11 / 09 08 07 06

Cover design by Brian Blount: www.webvisiongraphics.com
Page design by Mark Buschgens: www.markedbydesign.net

CONTENTS

FORWARD

I whole heartedly recommend to you Jerame Nelson's newest book "Activating God's Justice". You will be blessed and your heart enlightened helping you to understand more concerning the wonderful mercies of God. Do you feel ripped off by the enemy? John 10:10 tells us that the devil comes to steal, kill, and destroy, but Jesus came that we might have life and life more abundantly. In this book you will learn principles and receive keys that will help you overcome the attacks of the enemy and unlock a lifestyle of abundance in Christ. This book will help you tap into everything that God has called you to walk in and more as you learn to cry out to the Father of lights for 7-fold Justice. After reading this book you will want to recommend this book to all your friends. Not only do I endorse Jerame's book but I fully support all that he and his precious wife Miranda are doing to advance the Kingdom of God in the earth today.

Bobby Conner
Eagles View Ministries.

ACTIVATING THE JUSTICE OF GOD IN YOUR LIFE

Jesus came to the earth to take back what the enemy had stolen from His Father and restore to us the right to live out an abundant life. Jesus is ultimately, the God of Justice who revealed just how loved you are and how much life is yours to live. You have the right to activate the justice of God and take back seven-fold, what the enemy has stolen from your life and begin to live in the abundance of joy, peace, prosperity, and power that is your right as a son or daughter of God. Why live a defeated life? God never intended that we Christians, would live out defeated lives, being oppressed by the devil with no hope for a future or destiny. Jesus intended that we would live out an abundant life in which we would obtain peace, joy and righteousness that would cause us to have victory over the enemy at all times.

Let's get empowered!

I had a dream one night were God began to show me His plans to raise up an army of champions for His glory through the principles of justice.

In the dream, I was lying down in this huge room filled with about 20 bunk beds. The room had one big window in it, and the walls were made of cement. I knew that I was in an army barrack that housed the army of God. Soldiers were sleeping in their beds, resting for their next day of training. I could see their army fatigues and boots neatly folded at the foot of each bed.

I knew in the dream that I was in a place were God was raising up an army for Himself. It was a place of equipping and training like when a natural army goes through a time of boot camp to prepare for war.

I noticed that everyone was asleep except for me, and beside every bunk bed there was a night table containing peoples' personal belongings. As I looked closely to the left of my bunk I discovered a night table with a bunch of my personal stuff on it. I noticed three things on the table that belong to me - my wedding ring, my favorite watch, and my wallet. Then, just as I discovered this table with all of my personal belongings on it, I heard the sound of the one window in the room being forced open.

I watched as a man dressed all in black, with a black ski mask on covering his face, crawled through the window into the room. Then, all of a sudden, I realized that this man was a thief and he had broken in to the room to steal from the sleeping men. The thief did not notice me watching him. So, in the dream, I acted like I was asleep. Then, as I pretended to be asleep, I watched as the man began to steal everyone's personal stuff, moving from night table to night table, robbing people's personal items and putting them into this big sack.

All of a sudden the man headed strait for my stuff, and as he did, I jumped out of my bed and wrestled the man to the ground. I put him in a headlock and the man passed out. Then I noticed a phone that was in the room sitting on a table. I knew I needed to pick up the phone and report this thief to my authorities.

When I picked up the phone the scene changed and I was no longer in the bunkroom with the other solders but was now in a huge courtroom. I noticed a court case in progress. As I looked to the center of the room I saw that Jesus was there. He was beautiful and dressed in a judge's robe. I was amazed as I realized that I now stood before the righteous judge of all of heaven and earth. Then I realized that I was a part of this great trial and I also saw that the thief that I had wrestled down now standing in the room as well.

Jesus looked intently at the thief and declared, "You were caught in the very act. Now seven-fold justice must be recompensed." Jesus slammed down the court hammer and I watched as angels were sent immediately to bring his proclamation to pass. The vision ended with Jesus smiling at me as if I had won an amazing victory in God.

After I had the vision, I wrote it down and the Lord began to speak to me about the experience over a period of about one year. At times, I would close my eyes while in prayer about the meaning of the vision, and the Holy Spirit would take me back into the experience and reveal to me different truths about how God is raising up an army for Himself who would become mighty champions for His glory, and overcome the devil and his kingdom.

The first thing that God began to speak to me about through this dream was how He was raising up an army for His glory that would manifest His love and kingdom in the earth. He began to speak to me about how the body of Christ was in a time and season of being equipped and trained for war. That's why I was in an army barrack in my dream.

Then, He began to tell me that he was about to release new mantles of authority and power upon the body of Christ for the purpose of an end time harvest. He then said to me that the possessors of these mantles would be a generation who would walk in mighty demonstrations of his love and power like no other generation had before.

As He spoke this to me, I remembered the army fatigues and boots that were at the foot of the beds in my dream neatly folded and ready to be put to use. Then the Lord said to me "Those are the mantles that are to be given to those who are willing wake up out of their slumber and fight the good fight of faith."

After hearing all of this I asked the Holy Spirit,

"Where is all this at in the Bible? Where is there a connection between the army of God and His power"?

Then the Lord spoke to my spirit saying, *God's troops will willingly volunteer in the day of his power.* (See Psalm 110:3.)

As the Holy Spirit highlighted this to me I began to realize that now is not the time to be lukewarm and complacent, because God is about to awaken a generation to victory in the battle of light verses darkness. Then the Lord highlighted to me another verse: *Awake, awake and put on your strength, O Zion; Put on your beautiful garments, O Jerusalem, for the unclean and uncircumcised shall no longer come to you.* (Isaiah 52:1)

He began to show me that there was an entire generation who would began to walk victoriously over the devil and his kingdom through embracing the Justice of God.

He then spoke to me about how He was going to use the attacks of the enemy or the thief to empower his people to become stronger in the spirit than ever before. In fact, He showed me that they would not just overcome his attacks but that they would become stronger and stronger every time the enemy would attack; and that his people needed to begin to understand the principles of God's justice. I remembered the thief in the dream and how he came through the window to steal peoples' personal stuff. Then, I began to realize the importance of the words Jesus spoke to the thief. He said, "You have been caught in the very act. Let seven-fold justice be recompensed!"

I realized that I had heard these words before in the word of God. In scripture it says that when the thief is caught stealing from God's people he must repay sevenfold what has been taken (see Proverbs 6:30-31).

I knew that the Holy Spirit was giving me keys to overcome the enemy and his attacks as well as keys to step into being a part of His end time army. I realized that every one of us Christians have been attacked by satan and his evil hordes at one time or another, and every one of us has been ripped off in some way or another by the powers of darkness - in a personal way. As I was thinking about this, the Holy Spirit brought back to my memory the words of Jesus: *The thief does not come except to steal, and to kill, and to destroy. But I have come that they may have life, and that they may have it more abundantly* (John 10:10).

As the Lord began to speak to me through this scripture, I began to realize that Jesus came to the earth to take back what the enemy had stolen from His Father; as well as to restore to us, His people, the right to live out an abundant life. He came that we might have eternal life as well as victory over the devil in every way! As I began to get this revelation I realized that we are living in a time and day where, as the body of Christ, we cannot afford to allow the enemy to beat us up and steal from us any longer.

It is time for God's people to begin to stand up and fight the good fight of faith and no longer allow the enemy to have the upper hand. So many Christians live way below the means that the Father intended for them simply because they don't

understand God's word.

Psalms 97:1-6 lifts us to a higher way of thinking:

> *The LORD reigns; Let the earth rejoice; Let the multitude of isles be glad! Clouds and darkness surround Him; Righteousness and justice are the foundation of His throne. A fire goes before Him, And burns up His enemies round about. His lightnings light the world; The earth sees and trembles. The mountains melt like wax at the presence of the LORD, At the presence of the Lord of the whole earth. The heavens declare His righteousness, And all the peoples see His glory.*

This scripture shows us that the very foundations of God's throne are righteousness and justice. It shows us that God longs to declare his nature and goodness over his enemies. One of the key ways that God displays His rule and reign is through the Justice of God.

God never intended that we Christians, would live out defeated lives, being oppressed by the devil with no hope for a future or destiny. Jesus intended that we would live out an abundant life in which we would obtain peace, joy and righteousness that would cause us to have victory over the enemy at all times.

If we are to live out this abundant life we have to understand the Justice of God, and our rights as sons and daughters of God. You see, the enemy can't just run around doing what ever he pleases. He can only do what he has a legal right to do in the spirit. That however, does not stop him from overstepping his boundaries. Like I said earlier, the devil is a thief who comes to steal, kill, and destroy. He shows up in times when we least expect it, but we don't have to let him get away with it. What we need to do is learn how to deal with the enemy when he rears his head up and attacks. Just like in my vision we need to catch the thief in the very act of his attacks and call out to our authorities, which would be God, the father and the righteous judge - Jesus Christ.

An empowerment prayer to get you there:

Lord, show me where the enemy has ripped me off in my life, my friendships, family relationships and time and money. Release supernatural insight that will enable me to understand reclaim what was stolen. In the name of Jesus Christ, I command a blessing of favor, the right of a son and daughter of the King, to activate the justice of God in my life.

When have you felt like the enemy ripped your off in a particular relationship with a family member or significant other, or spouse? What would 7-fold justice look like to you?

If you believe that the enemy has ripped you off financially, what did he steal? And what would 7-fold recompense look like to you?

If you believe the enemy is ripping off your time and distracting you from focusing on Jesus, how would you begin to gain 7-fold justice and reclaim your time?

PERSIST UNTIL JUSTICE IS RELEASED

In my vision, the enemy came when all were asleep and began to steal people's stuff. When I jumped on him, I ended up receiving heaven's help as I called on my authorities from earth. God wants us to be victorious over the devil. Just like in the laws of the natural world and land, we have a right to claim justice in a court of law against those who have wronged us. We also have the right to receive justice from a court and system that's not of this earth. The key to receiving God's Justice is catching the thief in the act of his attack or recognizing when you have been illegally attacked, and then crying out to God for Justice about what your adversary has done to you. If we cry out, He will answer. We need to become like the persistent widow who cried out to the unrighteous judge for Justice and would not stop until he gave it to her.

Let's look at that parable.

> *Then He spoke a parable to them, that men always ought to pray and not lose heart, saying: 'There was in a certain city a judge who did not fear God nor regard man.*
>
> *Now there was a widow in that city; and she came to him, saying, 'Get justice for me from my adversary.'*
>
> *And he would not for a while; but afterward he said within himself, 'Though I do not fear God nor regard man, yet because this widow troubles me I will avenge her, lest by her continual coming she weary me.'*
>
> *Then the Lord said, 'Hear what the unjust judge said. And shall God not avenge His own elect who cry out day and night to Him, though He bears long with them? I tell you that He will avenge them speedily. Nevertheless, when the Son of Man comes, will He really find faith on the earth?'* (Luke 18:1-8)

In this story, Jesus admonishes us to not give up when things get hard but to continue praying even when things don't seem to go right and you seem to be under attack by the enemy. It's easy to pray a couple of times and then give up, but Jesus wants us to understand the persistent heart of the widow found in this parable. She did not relent from asking the unjust judge for justice. She eventually received it because of her continual asking. She asked so much that the unjust judge said to himself that he must give her justice least she weary me.

Then, Jesus went on to say that if the unjust judge would listen to the women's cry; how much more would the father in heaven listen to His own sons and daughters and speedily avenge them.

You see it's all about perspective.

God wants us to understand that if persistence worked in changing the unjust judge's heart, how much more will it move the heart of the father in heaven who loves his sons and daughters! Jesus even goes on to say that the Father longs to speedily avenge his own people as they cry out.

Sometimes we stop praying just short of a breakthrough. But the Word says: *Ask, and it will be given to you; seek, and you will find; knock, and it will be opened to you. For everyone who asks receives, and he who seeks finds, and to him who knocks it will be opened.* (Matthew 7:7-8.)

You see true faith has action behind it. It believes when you can't see and keeps going until God answers. That's why at the end of the story of the persistent widow, Jesus says in Luke 18:8, *When the Son of Man comes, will He really find faith on the earth?* God wants us to be persistent in prayer, and to not lose heart when we don't see the answer right away.

Daniel is a great example of persistence in prayer. In Daniel 10, we discover that he cried out day and night and even fasted for 21 days, until he finally got a breakthrough. The breakthrough came when the angel of the Lord appeared to him and told Daniel that the Lord had answered his prayer the very hour it was asked but the prince of Persia stood against him to oppose the answer from coming.

Sometimes the reason our prayers don't instantly get answered is because warfare comes against our prayer in the spirit. Ephesians 6:12 talks about this warfare: *For we do not wrestle against flesh and blood, but against principalities, against powers, against the rulers of the darkness of this age, against spiritual hosts of wickedness in the heavenly places.*

We must walk in persistence like Daniel did in prayer. If we will continually knock, seek, and ask, we will see our prayers answered. What would have happened if Daniel had given up on day 10 or even 20? We have to recognize our authority and rights as sons and daughters and ask God for the victory. We have to always keep in our hearts and minds, the fact that the Father is good and wants to do good for His sons and daughters.

There is power in prayer and it is a weapon that God has given us to overcome the devil. We see this in 2 Corinthians 10:3-4: *For though we walk in the flesh, we do not war according to the flesh. For the weapons of our warfare are not carnal but mighty in God for pulling down strongholds.* You see what we need to do is become like the persistent widow and recognize when we have been done wrong by our advisory the devil and continually cry for breakthrough until God answers.

Now let's look at another aspect of my Justice dream that pertains to what to ask God for justice for. God wants us to recognize first of all, when we have had things stolen from us. Then, we can make a demand on heaven to move in justice, forcing the hand of the enemy to restore what he took - 7-fold.

An empowerment prayer to get you there:

Lord, I see what has been stolen from me. And I ask for the ability to force the hand of the enemy to restore what he has taken. I cry out for breakthrough in me and through me. I come before you like the persistent widow asking for justice. I will not rest until I see breakthrough. Lord, show me how to pray and go to war for my inheritance.

When was the last time you felt moved to pray for days, weeks or months for something or someone in your life? What happened as a result of your prayers?

If you have never prayed persistently, fasting and seeking God for breakthrough, wisdom, strategy or favor, what would be most on your heart today – to ask God for?

Ask God for how you should pray to obtain justice in a matter most on your mind. Ask for His strategy for prayer and action and write it here:

PURSUE UNTIL RESTORATION HAPPENS

As I thought about the three items the enemy had tried to take, the Lord began to speak to me about each one. He began to tell me that each item had a symbolic meaning, which pertained to an aspect of justice that He wanted to begin to release to His people.

THE RING

First he began to speak to me about the ring. In the natural, the ring that was in my dream on the night table was my wedding ring. He began to tell me that the ring was a sign of covenant, that it had to do with relationships, and that it was His desire to began to restore things to the body of Christ in the area of relationships.

He then said, "Jerame, I want to began to restore relationships that the devil has stolen from my people. I want to restore back to my people who have suffered loss of friends and family for the gospel's sake."

As He said this, I thought about lost relationships with friends and family members that I had suffered since giving my life to Jesus. Holy Spirit began to remind me of Mark 10:29-30: *There is no one who has left house or brothers or sisters or father or mother or wife or children or lands, for My sake and the gospel's, who shall not receive a hundredfold now in this time—houses and brothers and sisters and mothers and children and lands, with persecutions—and in the age to come, eternal life.*

God wants to give us Justice in every area of our lives, especially in the area of relationships.

God wants heaven to invade earth and for circumstances to change in our lives regarding relationships; and, the best part is that He wants us to receive recompence and blessing now. He said that we would receive 100 fold in this lifetime, not one day far off in the future when we die and go to heaven.

It's time that we began to cry out to the righteous judge and began to ask for 7-fold justice, and even 100-fold justice, in the area of relationships, family, and friends that we have lost. Since the Lord began to show me that He wanted to restore relationships among His people I began to make a demand on heaven for my lost family members and friends who I had lost relationship with when I got saved. Then all of a sudden, childhood friends began to contact me and ask me about God. It was amazing how quickly it began to happen. I had had no contact with some of the individuals for years.

Justice in relationships can mean that those we know personally return to us and to the Lord. But 7-fold or 100-fold justice means that many more come along for the ride. One of the things we have gone after in our ministry over the years is souls. We have seen many decisions for Christ over the last 5 years and one of the ways we have tapped into seeing so many saved is that we began to ask the Lord for seven-fold Justice in the area of friends and family members we have lost who never came to know the Lord. We began to make a demand on God to release to us a soul winning anointing as well as open doors to preach the gospel and see people get saved. Since discovering God's heart for justice and crying out for it in the area of souls we have been to over 27 nations and seen over 30,000 decisions for Christ.

God does not want us to live defeated; He wants us to be victorious in all that we do.

You may have suffered the loss of family members or friends due not just to your faith, but lost them to sickness, or disease. One of the hardest things to experience and overcome as a Christian is a family member or friend dying from sickness or disease. Your faith takes a hard hit during times like this - unless you understand the power of God's love and Justice. God wants to give you justice. He wants you to tap into his Heart and overcome the attacks of the devil. One of the strongest attacks against the body of Christ is sickness and disease.

Many Christians who once lived in faith, that have had their faith in God rocked because of the loss of a family member. Many even lose faith in the supernatural power of God and His love, and have bought into the lies of the enemy. Lies like - God does not really love them, or that God is not really good. God wants to redeem his name and give to his people 7-fold justice in the area of death in the body of Christ.

There are far to many Christians who are dying yearly from sicknesses and diseases like cancer, and other life threatening conditions. We must put an end to these attacks of the enemy. Jesus said in Luke 10:19, that He has given us authority to trample on serpents and scorpions, and over all the power of the enemy, and nothing shall by any means hurt us. When this sort of thing happens to us we face one of two choices: The first is that we can buy into the plan of the enemy and doubt in the goodness and love of God's nature and character. Along the way, we lose all faith in the supernatural power of God to save, heal, and deliver. Or, you can take on the second choice and realize that sickness and disease is an attack from the devil and not something given from God to teach someone a lesson.

The key is to understand that the devil came to steal, kill and destroy; Jesus came that you might have life and life abundantly. This scripture shows us that the devil will steal or trespass in our lives if we let him, and there are times when he clearly crosses the line. When this happens we need to stand up and fight. We need to not have a victim mentality and give up but recognize that God is always good and he never changes. He is on our side! His goodness and love will not be mocked by the enemy.

Several years ago my Grandmother was diagnosed with terminal kidney cancer. She fought it for a long time and underwent chemotherapy. Then the cancer multiplied in the form of cancerous tumors, eventually spreading through out her whole body until she passed away. She died in her 60's. It was clearly premature. My family was devastated. My grandmother was like the glue that held our entire extended family together on my mom's side. Here we were, praying for her to get healed and the miracle never manifested.

I remember the temptation to be angry with God, and upset that she didn't get her miracle, and to begin to doubt His existence. But instead of allowing those feelings and temptations to get the best of me, I stirred up my faith. I just chose to believe that God is good. Even if I didn't understand why my grandmother was not healed.

A few years later, as I began to learn about the Justice of God I started making a demand on God for the death of my grandmother.

So I said to God, "Lord I want justice for this attack against my family and against my grandmother. I'm asking for 7-fold what was stolen from me. In fact God, I want a 7-fold anointing to destroy sickness and disease, and especially cancer and tumors."

I made my demand to God specific and grounded it in Proverbs 6:30-31: *People do not despise a thief if he steals to satisfy himself when he is starving. Yet when he is found, he must restore sevenfold; He must give all the substance of his house.*

Since that day I pulled on heaven and made a demand on the Scripture, declaring the power of His Word and promise, one of the miracles we have seen the most is people healed from terminal cancer and tumors. In fact we have seen over 20 cases of cancer healed since the death of my Grandmother. You see we have tapped into the Justice of God.

To some it may have looked like the devil might have won when my grandmother died but really her life became a seed that went into the ground to bring life to many.

I remember one night in Concord, North Carolina we were speaking at a meeting with about 1,000 people attending. During the worship, I went into an open vision where the Lord began to open my eyes to see what He intended to do that night in the miraculous. In the vision, I could see on the right side of the room 5 people with tumors and 4 others, over the left side. I watched as the fire of God burned them up. After the vision I asked the Lord what the vision meant and he told me that there where 5 women on the right side of the room with tumors or cysts on their breasts and 4 women on the left side of the room with the same condition. He told me to call them out and pray for them on the stage.

So at the beginning of the meeting, just after they had called me up to speak, I told the crowd my vision. I said, "If that's you, come up to the stage right now. God is going to heal you."

Exactly 5 came from the right and 4 women from the left. Then, as I laid my hands on their heads, one by one they began to be healed. Another woman saw them getting healed and she couldn't resist. She ran up to the stage to receive healing.

After we prayed, we asked the ladies to check privately to see if they were healed. One by one they came back and gave testimonies that God had healed them. All 10 women were healed that night from the tumors and cysts in the breast. God did exactly what he showed me - and more. He showed me 9 women with this condition and he went above and beyond and did 10. God is so good!

After the meeting had ended, I thought about the miracles that had taken place the Lord reminded me of my prayer for justice because of the death of my grandmother regarding cancer and tumors. It was then that I realized that God's goodness will always prevail over the attacks of the thief, and His justice will come though without fail.

Just recently, while preaching at a church in Kansas, I was sharing this revelation about my grandmother's death from cancer and the Justice of God. That night I felt the leading of the Lord to pray for everyone in the building who had cancer. As I gave the alter call, several women came forward for prayer. We ended up laying hands on them and declaring the 7-fold justice of God over them and rebuked the cancer in Jesus' name.

About a week later the pastor of that Kansas church called me. His voice sounded so excited as he went on to tell me that one of the women we had prayed for the last night of our meetings was touched mightily by God. He then went on to tell me that one of the women we prayed for to be healed of cancer felt better immediately after the meeting. Within a few days, she went in for her regular chemotherapy treatments and when she did, the doctors were shocked to discover that her tests showed no more cancer in her body. They even issued her a doctor's report stating that she was a miracle. God is good! This is one of the many reports that we have heard about as we have made a demand on God's justice in peoples live regarding cancer.

Are you one who has lost a love one prematurely to sickness and disease? Or are you one who has suffered the loss of your faith from an attack against a loved one who died? If so it's time to make a demand on the justice of God and ask the Lord Jesus for a 7-fold anointing to destroy sickness and disease. Ask him for opportunities to pray for those hurting with sickness and disease and see them healed. Remember be specific and make a demand on God for 7-fold.

If your faith has been shaken by the loss of a loved one or your trust in God's love has been hindered, then ask God for Justice in those areas. Ask him for sevenfold the faith and trust you lost, and watch as the Lord releases a radical gift of faith and trust that you never had before. God is Good!

An empowerment prayer to get you there:

Lord I ask you for 7 -old justice in every area of relationships that the devil has stolen from me. Lord, restore every place of attack with 7 -old blessing. Right now I call forth 7 times what the enemy has robed from me in the form of relationships. I pray for an anointing to see relationships restored, miracles happen, and souls to come into the kingdom in Jesus name. Amen.

If you have lost a loved one to disease or an accident, what would justice look like to you and God?

Have you ever prayed for someone to be healed? What happened? Ask God to increase your anointing to pray in such a way that the justice of God is released.

If you have been doubting the goodness of God because you believe God didn't stop something from happening, take a few minutes in quiet prayer and ask God to come and show you His goodness regarding that situation. Write down what you sensed that He showed you.

PLACE A DEMAND ON GOD AND REDEEM THE TIME

The second item on the night table that the thief tried to steal was my watch. After praying into the meaning of the watch the Lord began to speak to me about his desire to restore time that the devil had stolen from people.

THE WATCH

As He spoke this to me, I began to think about how so many people I knew had felt like the devil had stolen time from them and that they had missed their calling. I began to think about how even in my own life, when I first came to know the Lord, I had felt like the devil had stolen some of the best years of my youth. You see I didn't get saved until I was 22 years old, and I spent most of my younger days just getting drunk, and doing drugs, and being caught up in worldly living. After I met the Lord, I felt like I had really wasted away a lot of my life with carnal living. I thought if I could have just served the Lord in my younger years, the years would have been more awesome than what I had experienced. I could have traveled the nations preaching the gospel to the poor and walked out the great commission seeing souls won for Jesus. Then, about a year into being saved, I began to press into God and started developing a friendship with Him and all of the guilt and shame of the past that I had thought I had lost went away.

In the meanwhile, I kind of felt like the prodigal son that Jesus talked about who had wasted away his life with prodigal living. (Luke 15:11-31)

The Lord began to speak to me about time from God's point of view. God does not look at time the same way we do. In His Word it says that a day is but a thousand years and a thousand years is but a day to the Lord (2 Peter 3:8). God can make up time where we may feel like it has slipped away. What seems like an eternity for us could only be a moment of time in the eyes of the Lord.

It is nothing for God to make up lost time. God wants to take those who have felt like they have wasted their past and not accomplished much in life, and anoint them with a spirit of acceleration and Joy. Like He did with the prodigal son, He wants to place His robes of righteousness upon our lives, as well as give us a signet ring of sonship, and place the sandals of the gospel of peace upon our lives. He even wants to kill the fatted cow and have a big party in celebration that the old is gone and the new has come! God wants us to look forward to what is ahead and not what is behind us.

God wants us to place a demand on His Word and make a claim to regain the time that was stolen.

I began to make a demand on time that I felt was stolen from me. Shortly after I did, a spirit of acceleration came upon my life, and I was launched into full time ministry - after only being saved for 4 years. Since that time we have been in over 30 nations preaching the gospel of the kingdom seeing thousands come to know the Lord. God made up for the time I had felt I had lost because of my past mistakes.

No matter where you came from or what you have done, or how much time you think you have lost God is able to make up for it. Jesus wants us to know that our best days are ahead of us and not behind. Just like it says in Haggai 2:9 - *The glory of the latter temple shall be greater then the former, says the Lord and I will give you peace, says the Lord of hosts.*

God wants to give you peace if you think that time has slipped away from you. He wants the latter part of your life to be awesome! This goes for people of all ages. Even if you are 70-years-old, your better days can be ahead of you if you chose to believe and ask for sevenfold justice. So if you are one who feels that the devil has stolen time from you, cry out to God for Justice in this area. Ask Him to accelerate things in your life and to begin to make up for the time that the thief has stolen and watch what happens.

An empowerment prayer to get you there:

Lord, I pray that you would grant me 7-fold justice in every area of my life, especially in the area of time. I pray for an anointing of acceleration to come upon my life in every area that feels like its been wasted away and/or stolen from me. And I pray that the latter days of my life would be more glorious than the former in Jesus name. Amen.

When have you most felt like you were distracted from the things God asked you to do and time wasted away?

If you could go back and change that time, what would you have done differently?

At this stage of your life, what can you do now to reclaim your time and live in the fullness of the life God has for you?

RESTORING THE FAVOR OF GOD

The last thing on my nightstand was my wallet. As I prayed about the wallet, the Lord began to show me that my wallet represented the favor and finances of God as well as our identity in Christ. He then began to tell me that one of the areas He wanted to begin to give justice to the body of Christ was in the area of finances and favor. He said, "Jerame, I want to begin to restore to my people finances, lands, property and areas of business that went wrong because of the attacks of the devil."

THE WALLET

You see God wants to restore to his people 7-fold in every area of attack against their wallet or finances. If you were ripped of by the thief, you need to make your claim in the courts of heaven.

I believe the wallet is metaphorical for several things. In your wallet you can find all kinds of different stuff - like money, ID's, credit cards and, well, all sorts of personal stuff. I believe that all of these things are significant for what God is about to release - Justice to the body of Christ.

First let's talk about our ID cards and credit cards. These two things represent our identities in Christ and our credibility with people. They speak about the favor of God upon your life. God wants to restore identity and credibility with people who have experienced the pain of others who have talked falsely behind their backs and damaged their reputation. Some of you may have had people tell lies about you, or gossip behind your back. As a result, you may have lost favor in relationships or jobs or even a sense of who you are in the Lord for a season. God wants to bring justice to relationships. He is the God who gives us favor with Him as well as man.

The Bible says that Jesus "grew in favor with God and man" (Luke 2:52). This shows us that God knows that we, too, need favor and He will give us increased favor with man. If any of these things apply to you, it's time to call upon the righteous judge of the earth who sees all and knows all, to release to you 7-fold justice for what the enemy has done to you.

I remember a time when God gave us favor with an influential pastor in the UK who was fully speaking out against both of us and the move of the spirit that we were a part of. At the time, I was preaching in a big revival in a town called Dudley in the UK. This was a revival called the Dudley

Outpouring that lasted over 144 straight nights with over a 100,000 people attending the revival throughout that time.

I was blessed and privileged to have spoken during 20 of the nights of this revival. As we were ministering, God was doing many awesome miracles and hundreds of people were being saved, healed, and delivered. God was on the move and there was a big stir in the UK for revival at the time. But not everyone was happy about the revival.

There where many whose theology and background represented different circles or denominations than the church that had hosted the revival. They were openly criticizing the move of God and directly speaking against the things that God was doing; as well as against all of us who were preaching in the revival.

When this happened, I remember the Lord telling me, "Just bless those that persecute you and ask for Justice, for the battle does not belong to you but me." So that is what we did.

In fact, one of the biggest church leaders in all of the UK showed up to the meetings one night and it was my night to preach. I had no clue who the man was or that he had come to the meetings to personally check me out as well as the move of God. In fact, he had come to try to find some faults with the things I was preaching as well as with what God was sovereignly doing so that he could openly speak against the revival in order to discredit the things that God was doing there. I found out later that the man was a pastor of a church that had thousands of members and was one of the largest churches in the UK. At that time, he had only heard of the things that were happening in the move of God and had come to check it out. When he showed up he came with a whole group of His elders and stood in the back of the room to just watch what was going on.

As they watched that night, many people got gloriously healed and others saved! Then at the end of the meeting I gave an alter call for any leaders or pastors who wanted to receive an impartation of the Holy Spirit and power by the laying on of hands. As I gave the alter call, this pastor ended up telling his elders who were with him, "Come on, let's go up there and get in line for prayer. When we do, this guy is going to try to push us over when he prays for us and when he does, it will prove that this whole thing is of the flesh and not of God. Then, we will report it to our people and network to stay away from this false revival."

After the man said this, he came and stood in the middle of the prayer line with all the other leaders to receive an impartation of the Holy Spirit. As I went down the line to pray for people I would place my hand on the pastors' foreheads and release a prayer for more of the Holy Spirit. Some would be overwhelmed by the presence of God and fall over, others would shake, and others would just stand there not moving at all as the power of God was being released on them.

As I stepped towards the man who was expecting me to push him over, I heard the Holy Spirit say to me, "Don't lay your hands on his forehead but just barely touch his forehead with your pinky finger and pray."

So I did as the Lord told me, and when I barely touched the man with my pinky finger the power of God hit him so hard it actually knocked him off his feet and over the catcher that was behind him as if someone violently shoved him. He ended up taking out the first three rows of chairs on left the side of the room were he was standing. Then with out thinking, out of my mouth came this saying, "Bring that man up here now! He needs more of God's spirit than that for the calling of God he has on his life."

When I said that, the ushers picked the man up from the mess of scattered chairs and brought him to me and I ended up praying for him a second time. God continued to touch him. That night, this man who came to disprove the move of God, instead received the most powerful touch of God that he had ever experienced in his life.

I knew that that was the love of God towards that man as well as God backing up the move of His Spirit that was happening in that place. After praying for a few others that night we ended up closing the meetings and I never saw the man again.

Then, about two weeks later, I had lunch with one of the biggest church leaders in the UK right before doing some revival meetings in downtown London. This man went on to tell me about how I was now famous across the UK because of the pastor who had came to the revival to disprove it and got rocked. He then went on to tell me that the man who came had come to disprove the revival was one of the most influential leaders in the UK and that he publicly repented and began to tell everyone he knew that the move of God was legit and that my ministry was a genuine ministry of the Holy Ghost and revival.

He said to me that the man went from speaking against what God was doing in Dudley, as well as against my ministry, to becoming our biggest fan. In fact, because of that pastor and his testimony, over 1100 people packed the building we rented out that weekend in down town London. It was an awesome time in the presence of God and hundreds were healed and hundreds gave their lives to Jesus that weekend!

That weekend, God had turned around what seemed like an attack against our credibility and name, and caused the criticisms to fuel an even greater flame of revival. From the point on, we received over 30 invitations to speak all over the UK and have been back many times to the UK.

One of the things I learned through that experience was that we do not need to defend ourselves against the attacks of the enemy or of man. God is well able to defend his people and move on our behalf if we cry out to him for help and justice. God is able to restore your credibility with man even when things seem like that could be impossible.

You see, the Bible says to bless those that curse you or persecute you. In doing so, you actually give God a platform to bless you and deal with your critics or the enemy. As I was obedient to pray for God to bless that pastor and to administrate the Justice of God - God did marvelous things. Not only did He silence the voice of the accuser but He revealed

Himself to that pastor in a new way and broke him out of a religious box causing him to join in and promote what God was doing with revival in the UK!

Has the devil been attacking your credibility? Have people been speaking against your life, marriage or ministry? Or maybe you have been persecuted for what you are doing for God or what God is doing in your life? Don't fight with them and get into religious arguments. Look to the righteous judge of heaven and earth and began to Love and bless them and ask God for His Justice and watch him turn the situation around. This experience I went through showed me that God not only validated His move of the Spirit but He gave us major increase and favor and influence with leaders and pastors in the UK!

Once that attack is broken, you may just find other areas of your life and ministry being set free by the justice of God. And there is no greater pain than being attacked by either persons of influence or in the area of finances.

One of the other areas that God wants to release justice to His people in is in the area of finances. This was the first thing I thought about when I prayed about the meaning of the wallet. Many have been ripped of financially through loss of a job or someone stealing from you. Now is the time to ask God for Justice. I believe that we are living in a time and a day were, as the people of God, we must begin to recognize that God is our provider and not man. Even though the economic systems of this world may shake, we are not under the worlds system anymore. We are under God's economic system, and we live by his provision and what the word of God says.

God's word tells us that our father owns the cattle on a thousand hills, and that it's His will that we would be the lenders and not the borrowers, and the head and not the tail. We are living in a time and day when God is going to release justice for the hits that we have taken because of the world system we live in.

I remember a few years ago God began to speak to me about the finances of heaven. It happened while on a mission's trip to Indonesia, and Singapore. As my contact from Singapore dropped me off to send me to the airport he handed me a financial seed of blessing. He sowed 350 Singaporean dollars into me. As I arrived at the airport, I realized that I needed to buy a gift for my brother's wedding. I was going to be the best man a week after I returned to America. So, we checked our bags in at the airport and went through security and started looking for a gift in the Singapore airport. I found a guys-n-girls set of watches that I really liked and thought about buying them as a gift. The price of the watches was around 500 Singaporean dollars. As I was looking at the watches my friend told me he was hungry so I told the man working at the shop I would think about it and if I wanted to get the watches I would come back later.

So we went to eat some sushi, and after we did I decided to get the watches. While at dinner I explained to my friend that I wanted to get the watches and that I would have to use some US cash to pay for the watches along with the 350 dollars that my contact had given me. So we went back down to the watch shop and I told the guy working there I will take them. So he took them out and rang them up and they came up to around $497.64 Singaporean dollars. So I took out my 350 Singaporean dollars and started to count them out to give to the store clerk. As I did, I was surprised to find that I now had 400 Singaporean in my hands. So I told my friend, "I think my money just multiplied. Just a minute ago I only had 350 dollars and now I have 400."

My friend said to me, "Count it again." So I did and was shocked as the money multiplied again and went from 400 to 450. Then the store clerk who was watching this miracle also said count it again. So I counted it a third time and it multiplied to 500 Singaporean right in front of all three of us.

It was amazing! The money started multiplying right there as I was counting it. I started off with 350 dollars that I had counted many times and it multiplied to 500, and I was able to by the watches for my brother's wedding without having to use any of my own cash.

On my plane ride home from Singapore to LA, God spoke to me about this whole miracle. He asked "Jerame, don't you want to know what the sign of the multiplication of the finances means."

Then I said, "Yes Lord."

He replied, "You were buying watches for a bride and groom for a wedding and I want you to tell my people this. That it's a new time and a new season when the bride's groom from heaven is going to supernaturally provide for his bride on the earth to do all that she is called to do. Tell them that in this next season I am going to provide for my people and they must learn to trust me".

As God spoke this, I grew excited and realized that this sign of the money was much more then just a miracle - it was a message from God to me, and His people. After this happened, I asked Him where this all was in His word. I said, "Show me where you promised to supernaturally provide for all that your people are called to do."

The Holy Ghost led me to 2 Corinthians 9:8 - *And God is able to make all grace abound toward you, that you, always having all sufficiency in all things, may have an abundance for every good work.* I began to see that it was God's will for Him to provide for us, and not only was it His will, but He wanted to do it. As a bridegroom from heaven He wanted to release supernatural intervention on behalf of his bride, and cause her to tap into all that she needs, to do the things that God has called her to do.

God wants to provide for His bride! Especially when it comes to the things that He has called her to do. I have seen many times were God provided supernaturally for things that He called me to do for His name sake when things looked impossible for the provision in the natural.

I remember one time when God provided supernaturally for me to publish my first book with a major publication company when I had no money to do a project with them. It happened a few years ago that an amazing publishing company approached me out of the blue and offered me a contract to write a book with them. As I looked it over the contract, I noticed that it was super-expensive to publish a book under the co-publishing arrangement this big publishing company offered. But I felt like the expense would justify the distribution factor of the book. In fact, the book was going to cost me $14,000 dollars if I decided to sign the contract to do the book deal with them. Co-publishing an unknown or little known, first-time author is pretty much the norm for today's publishing industry. And I had a book on my heart that needed to be released.

At first, when I looked at the cost of the book, I was totally intimidated. But as I prayed, I felt the Holy Spirit tell me, "Don't worry about the cost of the book. If it's my will it's my bill. I want you to do the book."

As God said this to me it sparked faith in my heart to do the book. So that fall, I ended up signing the contract and wrote my first book. Then, within a few weeks of turning in the final manuscript, I received the first bill for the book. I began to get nervous as I read that I now owed the book company $14,000. I didn't have a single dollar to pay the company. In fact, I was just praying that I would be able to pay my mortgage that month much less pay a book company for a book. I could feel fear trying to grip me about this matter when the Holy Spirit spoke to me and reminded me about the promise that He gave me right before I signed the contract to write the book.

He said to me, "Son if it's my will, it's my bill. Don't be afraid. I am going to give you all the money for your book next week as you go to Indonesia for your missions trip."

This shocked me. I thought, *Lord are you really telling me that you are going to provide for my book by going on a missions trip that I am paying to go on to minister to your people?*

I remember thinking, *Wow God is going to provide for me $14,000 from a third world country.* Then I said, "Ok God, I believe."

About a week later, my wife Miranda and I flew off to Indonesia for a two-week evangelism tour. God blew us away with His favor and generosity. In almost every city we went to, random strangers and businessmen began to give us envelopes full of money. After two weeks of preaching the gospel in Indonesia I totaled up the funds and was blown away. The total amount of money that random people gave me was exactly $14,000 cash, in $100 US dollar bills. I was able to go home and pay my book off in full with the money and God did a mighty miracle for me just like He said to me that He would.

The awesome thing was that because I was able to pay off my first book by the time I wrote a second book, a year later, I had made enough profit on book sales from the first book to totally pay for the second book with no problems.

It was just like God told me in Singapore. - *And God is able to make all grace abound toward you, that you, always having all sufficiency in all things, may have an abundance for every good work.* See (2 Cor 9:8)

If it is His will, it's His bill. If we catch the vision of God for our lives we will also catch the provision as well. They come hand in hand. For some who are in a place of hope differed, you are heart-sick. You know that you have a vision that is of God for your life, but you are not experiencing the break-through that you need yet due to an attack of the enemy.

So if you are in a place were the enemy has stolen from you financially or you have lost favor, or reputation, now is you time to call upon the righteous judge of heaven and earth to release to you Justice. Don't allow bitterness to get into your heart and steal your provision. It's time to realize that the enemy wants to stop you from entering into your destiny. He wants to stop you from taping into heaven's supply over your life so that you never do what you are called to do in life. Forgive those who the devil has used as pawns in the chess game he plays against your life and ask justice from your bridegroom in heaven who is the righteous judge and watch him avenge His people with 7-fold.

You see, God wants to restore to his people 7-fold in every area of attack against their wallet or finances. If you were ripped of by the thief, you need to make your claim in the courts of heaven. There are some in the body of who have been involved in business projects that went sideways. God wants to give you back what has been taken from you. It's time to begin to cry out to God to restore what has been taken from you and ask for greater opportunities to come your way. Now is a time of advancement. While the world is under the curse of the world system, you are not. You are under the blessings and favor of your Father in heaven, and its time to recognize it. So take some time to spend with the Lord and allow him to show you the areas in your life were He wants to give you justice and begin to make decrees and prayers to the Lord for 7-fold what has been stolen from you.

An empowerment prayer to get you there:

Father, I pray for Justice in the area of credibility, identity and finances in my life. Lord, grant me Justice in every place of my life where the devil has tried to ruin my credibility and steal my favor with people and also the provision to do what you have called me to do. Lord , I pray for those who have been used by the enemy to persecute and speak against what you are doing in my life. I pray blessings over them in Jesus' name. Open their hearts to know you more and grant to me Justice on behalf of their attacks. Right now, I decree a 7-fold increase of favor, finances, and credibility in my life in Jesus name. Amen.

Was there ever a time when someone spoke unjustly against you? What did you see God do to change the situation? If He has not changed the situation, what might He be asking you to do?

Was there ever a time when you have unjustly spoken against others? What is God asking you to do to make amends? Sometimes a simple prayer of acknowledgement will release you from the past and make space for you to receive the justice of God. Sometimes, you may need to go to that person and ask forgiveness. Forgiveness changes the atmosphere and enables justice to be released.

Write out a decree that is based on scripture, that will cause the enemy to back off and release space for the Justice of God to intervene in a relationship or a financial situation. Then speak it out!

72 ACTIVATING THE JUSTICE OF GOD IN YOUR LIFE

ABOUT JERAME NELSON

Jerame Nelson is the founder of Living at His Feet Ministries. He is an author, as well as a well-known international conference speaker and a crusade revivalist to the nations. It's Jerame's passion to equip the body of Christ in the areas of hearing God's voice, as well as walking in the supernatural power of God in everyday life. Jerame and his wife, Miranda, live in San Diego, California, and work together in the ministry to change the lives of thousands through the Gospel of Jesus Christ.

PRODUCTS

Other products by Jerame include:

Manifesting God's Love through Signs, Wonders, and Miracles
(Destiny Image Publishers, 2010)

Burning Ones: Calling forth a Generation of Dread Champions
(Destiny Image Publishers, 2011)

Come into the Glory: A Techno Experience

Activating Your Spiritual Senses

CONTACT

For more information on the ministry and writings of Jerame Nelson go to: www.livingathisfeet.org

Address:

Living At His Feet Ministries
591 Telegraph Canyon Rd. Suite 705
Chula Vista, CA 91910

Email: admin@livingathisfeet.org
Follow Jerame Nelson on Twitter at: @jeramenelson

CPSIA information can be obtained at www.ICGtesting.com
Printed in the USA
LVOW06s0416030614

388332LV00002B/29/P